A Gift of

The Wellesley
Free Library
Centennial Fund

VIRTUAL FIELD TRIPS

# COLONIAL WILLIAMSBURG

## A MyReportLinks.com Book

# Wim Coleman and Pat Perrin

MyReportLinks.com Books

an imprint of

 Enslow Publishers, Inc.

Box 398, 40 Industrial Road
Berkeley Heights, NJ 07922
USA

MyReportLinks.com Books, an imprint of Enslow Publishers, Inc. MyReportLinks®
is a registered trademark of Enslow Publishers, Inc.

Copyright © 2005 by Enslow Publishers, Inc.

**Library of Congress Cataloging-in-Publication Data**

Coleman, Wim.
  Colonial Williamsburg / Wim Coleman & Pat Perrin.
    p. cm. — (Virtual field trips)
  Includes bibliographical references and index.
  ISBN 0-7660-5220-6
  1.  Colonial Williamsburg (Williamsburg, Va.)—Juvenile literature. 2.  Williamsburg (Va.)—History—
Juvenile literature. I. Perrin, Pat. II. Title. III. Series.
  F234.W7.C55 2005
  975.5'4252—dc22
                                   2004003547


Printed in the United States of America

10 9 8 7 6 5 4 3 2 1

**To Our Readers:**
Through the purchase of this book, you and your library gain access to the Report Links that specifically back
up this book.
The Publisher will provide access to the Report Links that back up this book and will keep these Report Links
up to date on **www.myreportlinks.com** for five years from the book's first publication date.
We have done our best to make sure all Internet addresses in this book were active and appropriate when we
went to press. However, the author and the Publisher have no control over, and assume no liability for, the
material available on those Internet sites or on other Web sites they may link to.
The usage of the MyReportLinks.com Books Web site is subject to the terms and conditions stated on the
Usage Policy Statement on **www.myreportlinks.com**.
A password may be required to access the Report Links that back up this book. The password is found on the
bottom of page 4 of this book.
Any comments or suggestions can be sent by e-mail to comments@myreportlinks.com or to the address on
the back cover.

**Photo Credits:** APN Media, LLC, p. 26; Clipart.com, pp. 1, 3, 16, 19, 20, 24, 29, 30, 33; © Corel
Corporation, pp. 14, 15, 41; Enslow Publishers, Inc., p. 9; Library of Congress, p. 28; Library of
Congress/Kurz & Allison, Chicago, p. 37; Park Net, the National Park Service, p. 39; Mary Ann Sullivan,
pp. 17, 23; MyReportLinks.com Books, p. 4; Oil painting by Charles Wilson Peale, 1791, p. 31; The Colonial
Williamsburg Foundation, pp. 10, 35; Virginia Historical Society, p. 12.

**Cover Photo:** Painet, Inc.

**Cover Description:** The Governor's Palace and an actor in period clothing.

# MyReportLinks.com Books
## Great Books, Great Links, Great for Research!

The Internet sites listed on the next four pages can save you hours of research time. These Internet sites—we call them "Report Links"—are constantly changing, but we keep them up to date on our Web site.

Give it a try! Type http://www.myreportlinks.com into your browser, click on the series title, then the book title, and scroll down to the Report Links listed for this book.

The Report Links will bring you to great source documents, photographs, and illustrations. MyReportLinks.com Books save you time, feature Report Links that are kept up to date, and make report writing easier than ever!

Please see "To Our Readers" on the copyright page for important information about this book, the MyReportLinks.com Web site, and the Report Links that back up this book.

Please enter **FTC1852** if asked for a password.

The Internet sites described below can be accessed at
http://www.myreportlinks.com

*EDITOR'S CHOICE

▶Colonial Williamsburg

Experience Colonial Williamsburg through the images found on this
Web site, and learn about how people lived in colonial times.

*EDITOR'S CHOICE

▶The College of William & Mary

At the College of William and Mary Web site you can learn the history
of America's second oldest college. You will also learn about Thomas
Jefferson, one of the college's former students.

*EDITOR'S CHOICE

▶Colonial Williamsburg Tour

At this Web site you can take a virtual tour of Colonial Williamsburg.
Click on the different areas of the interactive map to learn more about
each destination.

*EDITOR'S CHOICE

▶Williamsburg, Virginia

Explore images of Colonial Williamsburg's extraordinary architecture,
including images of Bruton Parish Church, the Capitol, Carter's Grove,
and many other historic locations.

*EDITOR'S CHOICE

▶Becoming Americans

The Virginia Historical Society explores the causes of the American
Revolution and the drafting of the Declaration of Independence.

*EDITOR'S CHOICE

Virginia and the American Revolution

At this Web site you will learn about Virginia's role in the American
Revolution and how the First Continental Congress came to be.

## Report Links

### The Internet sites described below can be accessed at http://www.myreportlinks.com

▶ **Africans in America: Revolution**

The Africans in America Web site explores the roles of Africans in the United States from 1450 to 1865.

▶ **The American Revolution: Lighting Freedom's Flame**

Learn about the American Revolution through virtual tours of historic places, biographies of participants in the war, and much more at the National Park Service Web site.

▶ **Archiving Early America**

The Archiving Early America Web site explores life in colonial times through historic documents, writings, maps, portraits, and events.

▶ **Charters of Freedom**

At the National Archives Web site you can read and learn about the Declaration of Independence, the Constitution, and the Bill of Rights.

▶ **Colonial National Historical Park**

The National Park Service Web site provides a brief description of Colonial National Historical Park. Click on "In Depth" to learn more about this historic location.

▶ **Colonial Williamsburg**

At the American Park Network Web site you will find many useful resources about Colonial Williamsburg, including a concise history, photography, and a listing of sites to see.

▶ **Colonial Williamsburg: Tour the Town**

This site provides a unique look at Colonial Williamsburg. Click on the different areas of the town to learn more about the buildings and the people who lived there.

▶ **Creating a Virginia Republic**

At this Library of Congress Web site you can learn about Thomas Jefferson's vision to create an ideal republic in Virginia.

## Report Links

### The Internet sites described below can be accessed at http://www.myreportlinks.com

▶**From Revolution to Reconstruction**

This Web site contains a collection of documents from the colonial era, including the Stamp Act and the Peace Treaty of Paris.

▶**Hampton Roads History Tour: Bruton Parish Church**

Read a brief history of the Bruton Parish located in Williamsburg, Virginia, at this Web site.

▶**House of Burgesses**

Learn about the origins of the House of Burgesses and about some of its members, including George Washington and Thomas Jefferson.

▶**Jefferson and the Capitol**

From the Library of Virginia you can learn about Thomas Jefferson and his plans for the Capitol building in Virginia.

▶**John D. Rockefeller, Jr.**

The National Park Service Web site has a profile of John D. Rockefeller and his contributions to restoring Colonial Williamsburg.

▶**Jump Back in Time: Colonial America (1492–1763)**

America's Story from America's Library, a Library of Congress Web site, tells the story of colonial America. Here you will learn about Jamestown and other colonies of early Virginia.

**Jump Back in Time: Revolutionary Period (1764–1789)**

America's Story from America's Library, a Library of Congress Web site, tells the story of the American Revolution. Interesting stories related to this period are included.

**Liberty!**

This PBS Web site lets Web users explore the American Revolution through headlines, time lines, and photo essays. Learn about what it was like to live in the colonial era.

## Report Links

▶ **Map Collections: 1500–2003**

At this Library of Congress Web site you can explore maps from the 1500s
through 2003.

▶ **The Papers of George Washington**

The Papers of George Washington Web site has a collection of letters written
by America's first president on the topic of the revolution.

▶ **Powder Magazine in Williamsburg**

The Powder Magazine in Williamsburg, Virginia, was first built by the British
to hold military supplies. The Virginia Historical Society Web site tells the story
behind this historic structure.

▶ **Related Information**

At the U.S. History.org Web site you can explore information relating to events
leading up to the colonies' declaration of independence from Great Britain.

▶ **The *Virginia Gazette***

The *Virginia Gazette* first went to print in Williamsburg in 1736. It was the first
newspaper in the colonies. View its articles at this site.

▶ **Virginia Historical Society**

At the Virginia Historical Society you can explore the society's many online exhibits
detailing Virginia's long history.

▶ **A Virtual Colonial Town**

Take a virtual tour through Colonial Williamsburg. Learn about the importance of
certain places, view images of historic locations, and learn what it was like to live in
the colonial era.

▶ **Williamsburg Postcards**

View a collection of postcards from Williamsburg, Virginia, at this Web site. See images
of historic locations, and learn about the publishers and printers that created them.

Virginia was a British colony from its founding in 1607 to its ratification, or acceptance, of the Declaration of Independence in 1776.

The first Virginia capital was Jamestown, the first permanent English settlement in the New World.

For the new capital, Virginia's leaders chose a community named Middle Plantation. It was named Middle Plantation because this community was in the middle of the Virginia peninsula formed by the James and York rivers.

Middle Plantation was renamed Williamsburg in honor of King William III of England.

Williamsburg was the capital of Virginia from 1699 until 1780.

In the early twentieth century, Williamsburg was restored to its eighteenth-century appearance.

The restoration of Colonial Williamsburg was funded by John D. Rockefeller, Jr. Williamsburg is now operated by the Colonial Williamsburg Foundation, a nonprofit educational organization.

Today, the Williamsburg Historic Area covers more than 170 acres. It includes more than eighty original buildings from the 1700s.

Visitors can talk to historical interpreters playing the parts of colonial citizens and take part in the reenactment of colonial activities.

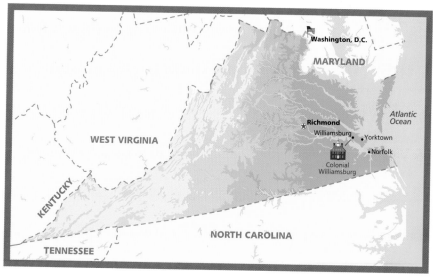

▲ A map of Virginia.

## Chapter 1 ▶

# The Sword Is Drawn!

**One** spring night more than two hundred years ago, most of the people in Williamsburg, Virginia, were fast asleep in their beds. Captain Henry Collins, though, and his company of Royal Marines were wide-awake. They were sneaking through the darkness toward the town's Powder Magazine—the building where weapons and gunpowder were stored.[1]

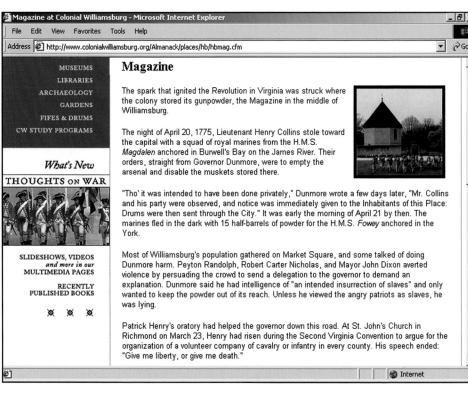

Magazine at Colonial Williamsburg - Microsoft Internet Explorer

File    Edit    View    Favorites    Tools    Help

Address http://www.colonialwilliamsburg.org/Almanack/places/hb/hbmag.cfm    Go

MUSEUMS
LIBRARIES
ARCHAEOLOGY
GARDENS
FIFES & DRUMS
CW STUDY PROGRAMS

*What's New*

THOUGHTS ON WAR

SLIDESHOWS, VIDEOS
*and more in our*
MULTIMEDIA PAGES

RECENTLY
PUBLISHED BOOKS

### Magazine

The spark that ignited the Revolution in Virginia was struck where the colony stored its gunpowder, the Magazine in the middle of Williamsburg.

The night of April 20, 1775, Lieutenant Henry Collins stole toward the capital with a squad of royal marines from the H.M.S. *Magdalen* anchored in Burwell's Bay on the James River. Their orders, straight from Governor Dunmore, were to empty the arsenal and disable the muskets stored there.

"Tho' it was intended to have been done privately," Dunmore wrote a few days later, "Mr. Collins and his party were observed, and notice was immediately given to the Inhabitants of this Place: Drums were then sent through the City." It was early the morning of April 21 by then. The marines fled in the dark with 15 half-barrels of powder for the H.M.S. *Fowey* anchored in the York.

Most of Williamsburg's population gathered on Market Square, and some talked of doing Dunmore harm. Peyton Randolph, Robert Carter Nicholas, and Mayor John Dixon averted violence by persuading the crowd to send a delegation to the governor to demand an explanation. Dunmore said he had intelligence of "an intended insurrection of slaves" and only wanted to keep the powder out of its reach. Unless he viewed the angry patriots as slaves, he was lying.

Patrick Henry's oratory had helped the governor down this road. At St. John's Church in Richmond on March 23, Henry had risen during the Second Virginia Convention to argue for the organization of a volunteer company of cavalry or infantry in every county. His speech ended: "Give me liberty, or give me death."

Internet

▲ *The Powder Magazine building was a place where the people of Williamsburg stored gunpowder around the time of the Revolutionary War. When the colonists learned the British governor tried to steal the gunpowder, it became one of the issues that led them to rebel.*

The marines broke into the Powder Magazine. They smashed the muskets that were stored there.

Then the Royal Marines lifted the half-barrels of gunpowder— fifteen in all—and lugged them out of the building. They put the barrels on a wagon and moved them to a British ship.[2]

The marines, however, were not the only ones awake that night of April 20, 1775. One of the Williamsburg townspeople spotted the thieves at work. He hurried to tell others, and they called out the town drummers. Very soon, the sound of beating drums was heard in every part of town.[3] By dawn, an angry crowd had gathered in Market Square to protest the theft.[4]

## What Was All the Fuss About?

The marines were British, and they were acting on orders from the British governor of Virginia, John Murray, Earl of Dunmore. The governor even provided the wagon to carry the barrels.[5]

In April 1775, the people who lived in Williamsburg were British, too. Virginia was one of the thirteen American colonies that belonged to Great Britain. So why were British marines stealing gunpowder from British citizens?

When the town leaders asked Governor Dunmore that question, he made excuses. He said that he had heard of a planned slave rebellion, so he thought it best to remove the gunpowder to a safer place.[6]

The real reason the governor took the gunpowder was quite different. The governor was afraid the colonies would rebel. For several years, the American colonies had protested against new taxes and laws made by Great Britain. Virginia leader Patrick Henry had made fiery speeches in Williamsburg against British taxes.

In March 1775, Henry had made a speech in Richmond that ended with the words, "Give me liberty, or give me death." That now-famous line was at least part of the reason why Dunmore sent the marines sneaking around in the dark to steal gunpowder.[7]

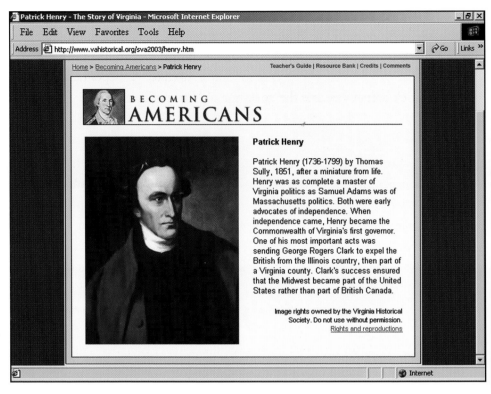

Home > Becoming Americans > Patrick Henry

Teacher's Guide | Resource Bank | Credits | Comments

BECOMING
AMERICANS

**Patrick Henry**

Patrick Henry (1736-1799) by Thomas Sully, 1851, after a miniature from life. Henry was as complete a master of Virginia politics as Samuel Adams was of Massachusetts politics. Both were early advocates of independence. When independence came, Henry became the Commonwealth of Virginia's first governor. One of his most important acts was sending George Rogers Clark to expel the British from the Illinois country, then part of a Virginia county. Clark's success ensured that the Midwest became part of the United States rather than part of British Canada.

Image rights owned by the Virginia Historical Society. Do not use without permission.
Rights and reproductions

▲ The incident at the Powder Magazine building shortly followed Patrick Henry's famous speech where he proclaimed "Give me liberty, or give me death!"

Meanwhile, similar things were happening farther north. A few days after the raid on the Powder Magazine, word came that British soldiers had tried to seize weapons and gunpowder in the Massachusetts towns of Lexington and Concord. Shots had been fired, and men had been killed on both sides.

The *Virginia Gazette* proclaimed, "The Sword is now drawn and God knows when it will be sheathed."[8] The *Virginia Gazette* was the colony's first newspaper, started in Williamsburg in 1736.

Those battles in Massachusetts marked the beginning of the Revolutionary War, in which the American colonies won their independence from Great Britain. Angry over the theft of their gunpowder, Virginia colonists were ready to fight.

In June, Patrick Henry led 150 military men toward Williamsburg, threatening the governor.[9] Governor Dunmore fled to a British ship, and the Virginia colony was on its own.[10]

In 1776, when the United States declared independence, Patrick Henry became the governor of Virginia.

## The Powder Magazine

One can visit the Powder Magazine in Williamsburg today. It is a tall, octagonal (eight-sided) building, just as it was originally built in 1715. The wall around it and the Guardhouse were added in the mid-eighteenth century. After the colonies won the Revolutionary War, the Powder Magazine became less important for storing weapons. Over the following years, it was used as a Baptist meetinghouse, a dance school, and a stable for horses.

Today the Powder Magazine holds an exhibit of weapons—colonial swords, handguns, and rifles. Actors and reenactors are on hand throughout Colonial Williamsburg to answer visitors' questions. Weapon makers and guards tell visitors about colonial military life.[11] Visitors might even be asked to join a "bucket brigade" passing along buckets of water to fill the colonial-style fire engine that is kept near the Guardhouse.[12]

## Market Square and the Courthouse

The Powder Magazine is in Market Square, the place where townspeople gathered at dawn to protest the gunpowder theft. The square is an open area that extends on both sides of Williamsburg's main street, Duke of Gloucester Street (pronounced Gloss-ter).

In colonial times, farmers brought their produce to Market Square early each morning. They put out their vegetables, milk, butter, cheese, eggs, fruit, meat, and seafood for sale. Housewives and cooks came to shop. Games, horse races, and fiddling contests were held in or near the square. Market Square is also where land and African-American slaves were sold.[13]

Across the street from the Powder Magazine building is the Courthouse, where colonial townspeople came to see neighbors on trial for such things as cheating at cards, stealing livestock, or being in debt.[14] More serious crimes were tried by the Virginia court in the Capitol building. Those convicted of local crimes were often taken outside the Courthouse for immediate punishment.

Since 1662, Virginia had required every town to have a whipping post, ducking stool, stocks, and a pillory for punishing criminals.[15] Today, a whipping post stands near the Courthouse like the one that had been there in colonial times.

▲ The Courthouse is located across the street from the Powder Magazine building. The Courthouse was the scene of public trials and punishments.

During the revolutionary era, the Williamsburg Militia Company would perform drills in front of the Courthouse. In modern times, visitors watch reenactments of the drills.

For punishing less serious offenses, prisoners were put into the stocks or pillory. Stocks and pillory are wooden structures that hold a prisoner in place by the ankles or the neck and wrists. Offenders were held by the authorities while others made fun of them.[16] Today, visitors can try out the stocks and pillory at the Courthouse. Or they might play the part of a defendant, witness, or judge in the trials that are reenacted there.[17]

In 1776, townspeople heard the Declaration of Independence read from the steps of the Courthouse. In 1783, they gathered there again to hear that Great Britain had agreed to the terms of the peace treaty that ended the Revolutionary War.

Several times each year, the Williamsburg Militia Company trained near the Courthouse. The townspeople would gather to watch them perform drills.[18]

Today, actors in colonial uniform hold drills with guns and bayonets as soldiers would have in the 1700s. Visitors can join in the fun during these reenactments. It is all part of the living museum that is Colonial Williamsburg.

**Chapter 2** ▶

# Everyday Life on the Great Street

**From** 1699 to 1780, Williamsburg was the capital of the Virginia colony. At that time, Virginia was mostly made up of plantations and smaller farms. Williamsburg was the colony's most important town.[1]

Williamsburg was the home of the British governor of Virginia. The two governing bodies made up of colonists—the Council and the House of Burgesses—met there, too. Students from well-to-do Virginia families attended the College of William and Mary located in town.

▲ *The Virginia courts tried people for serious crimes in Williamsburg. Sometimes the punishment would be that the person was put in the pillory. These visitors show what this may have been like.*

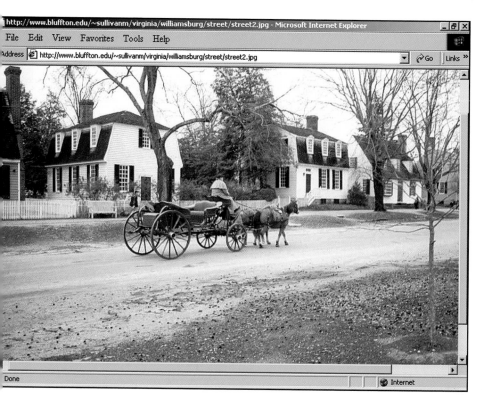

```
http://www.bluffton.edu/~sullivanm/virginia/williamsburg/street/street2.jpg - Microsoft Internet Explorer    _ ☐ ✕
File    Edit    View    Favorites    Tools    Help
Address 🖉 http://www.bluffton.edu/~sullivanm/virginia/williamsburg/street/street2.jpg          ▼  🔗 Go   Links »
Done                                                                              🌐 Internet
```

▲ *Duke of Gloucester Street is the main street of Colonial Williamsburg. This carriage is going past some of the nicer houses in town.*

Although only an estimated two thousand people lived in Williamsburg, many others came for business, social, and cultural events.[2] Four times a year, Virginia courts tried serious crimes in Williamsburg. Then crowds of people filled the town, including those who took part in the trials and those who came to see what happened. The highest court, the General Court, met in April and October. The General Court drew such crowds that the days when it met were known as "Publick Times."[3]

Due to the fact that Williamsburg attracted the colony's wealthy and important citizens, it also attracted many merchants and craftspeople. They opened shops and sold a great variety of goods, especially in Market Square and along Duke of Gloucester Street.

## Duke of Gloucester Street

Williamsburg's 99-foot-wide Duke of Gloucester Street runs through the heart of the town—between the Capitol building at the east end and the college at the west end. In the eighteenth century, it was usually called "the main street" or "the great street."[4]

George and Martha Washington, Thomas Jefferson, Patrick Henry, James Madison, and many other founders of the United States once walked or rode along the great street. Townspeople and foreign visitors hurried up and down the street, carrying on their business.

Plantation owners drove their fancy carriages down Duke of Gloucester Street when they came to town. The colonial governor might ride by in a coach drawn by six matching horses.[5] Farmers drove more ordinary wagons, taking their produce to market. Sometimes American Indians came to discuss treaties with British officials, or to trade and sell their crafts.

Those who traveled Duke of Gloucester Street could find the trip rather difficult. Mud in the great street was sometimes about two feet deep. Chickens, sheep, cattle, and other livestock wandered about freely.[6] At one time, a herd of ponies grazed wherever it wanted.[7] People building houses along the street were asked to put up fences to keep stray cattle out of their gardens, but that did not keep animals out of the street.[8]

Now, the great street is paved, cleaner, and free from roaming animals and mud. Visitors can walk or ride in horse-drawn carriages. Strolling along Duke of Gloucester Street today, visitors find shops where people make and sell their wares just as local craftspeople did many years ago.

## Craftspeople at Work

Colonial-style shops still line Market Square, Duke of Gloucester Street, and other nearby streets. Craftspeople go about their jobs, using eighteenth-century tools and skills. Anyone can visit their shops and watch them at work.

Guests might see a silversmith making bowls and cups, or a milliner stitching up the latest in colonial fashions. The wigmaker uses horse, goat, and human hair to create stylish wigs and pin-on curls. The apothecary shop displays colonial cures for toothaches and other ailments.

The Printing Office and Bookbindery print copies of colonial newspapers on old-style presses. At one end of the great street, near the Capitol building, a gunsmith turns iron, steel, brass, and wood into weapons.

Activities from colonial days are still being performed on nearby streets, including shoemaking, brickmaking, and carpentry. A wheelwright makes wheels for carts and carriages. A cooper makes casks and other wooden containers.

Colonial blacksmiths used to make horseshoes and armor. Blacksmiths working in Williamsburg today make tools, nails, and household hardware such as hinges and latches. At the foundry, workers cast objects in bronze, brass, pewter, and silver. A cabinetmaker uses tools to make furniture and harpsichords, a keyboard instruments similar to a piano. A harpsichord's strings are plucked rather than struck.

In Williamsburg, people also still work at crafts such as basketry and cider making. A windmill, once used to grind grain into flour, is open to visitors.

*There are currently blacksmiths working in Colonial Williamsburg in much the same way they worked in the late 1700s.*

## The College of William and Mary

At the west end of the great street is the College of William and Mary, the second oldest college in the United States. (Harvard University is the oldest.)[9] In 1693, the British founded the college at Middle Plantation to provide a religious and traditional education for colonists and American Indians. The college included a grammar school, where boys could begin their studies at age twelve. There was also a philosophy school and a divinity school. As time went by, both the religious connections and grammar school were dropped.[10]

The boys studied Latin and Greek, languages that were believed to be important in a proper education. Classes were taught in Latin, and students had to do their written work in Latin, too.

They studied mathematics and geography, and practiced their handwriting skills. Older students learned subjects such as physics, law, chemistry, medicine, and modern languages.

Thomas Jefferson, James Monroe, and other important colonial leaders studied at the College of William and Mary. George Washington was never a student at the College of William and Mary, but he served as chancellor, or head official, of the school.[11]

The Wren Building is part of the College of William and Mary. It is the oldest academic building in the country that still holds classes.

The colonists who went to the College of William and Mary were mostly boys from well-to-do families. Higher education was not considered important for girls, and education of any kind was not available to slaves. American Indian students were expected to live like Englishmen, so that they could in turn teach their people. Many of the American Indian students became translators between their nations and the colonists, but few actually changed their lifestyles.[12]

## The Wren Building

The Wren Building on the College of William and Mary campus was built in 1705. It is the oldest academic building in America that is still in use.[13] The building is named for Christopher Wren, a famous royal architect. Most historians do not believe that Wren actually designed the building, although he might have influenced its design.

Several times, the Wren Building was partly destroyed by fire, and rebuilt. Its design was changed each time that it was rebuilt. In the 1930s, it was restored to its original design.

At first, the Wren Building held William and Mary's grammar school. The building, however, was not limited to educational use. The Virginia General Assembly met there for a few years while the Capitol building was constructed, and again while the Capitol was being rebuilt after a fire. In the early years, a dance teacher rented one of the Wren Building classrooms for his classes. During the Revolutionary War, British General Charles Cornwallis used it as his headquarters. Then French General Rochambeau, who was fighting on the American side of the war, used the Wren Building for a while as well.

Today, students at the College of William and Mary still go to classes in the Wren Building. Guests can visit the first floor to see how the school looked in colonial days.[14]

**Chapter 3 ▶**

# British Nobility and Virginia Gentry

**Before** the American Revolution, the colony of Virginia was controlled by the British government. The colonists admired and copied British houses, clothing, and government. Wealthy colonists adopted the manners of British nobility. Well-to-do colonists usually sent their sons to be educated in England.

When Williamsburg became the capital of the Virginia colony in 1699, the colonists wanted to build a town they could be proud of.[1] According to British ideas of that time, a city should be the center of education, religion, and politics. It should have grand open areas for public use.[2]

Francis Nicholson was the governor of Virginia from 1698 to 1705. He laid out the plan of Williamsburg, arranging the streets and major buildings with those ideas in mind.[3] The College of William and Mary was already the town's educational center. A community church would become the religious center. The Capitol would be one political center. A house built for British governors would be another political center.

The governor's house was not finished while Nicholson was in office so he did not get to live in it. Nicholson, though, seems to have given special attention to where the house would be placed.

## ▶ Palace Street

On the north side of Duke of Gloucester Street, near Market Square, is Palace Street. The street's two lanes are divided by a

▲ *Palace Street comes to an end at the Governor's Palace. The original building was completed in 1722.*

long, open area called the Palace Green. At the far end of that green is the Governor's Palace.

Around 1718, the first theater in America opened on Palace Street. Plays were popular in Williamsburg, and several theaters put on amateur and professional productions.[4] Today, actors present scenes from colonial plays in an open-air theater on Palace Street. Visitors can also see shops on Palace Street, much like the ones that were there in colonial days.

Early in the eighteenth century, townspeople began building homes along Palace Street. At first, these houses were simple, with just two or three rooms per floor. That changed over time.

## The Thomas Everard House

John Brush, the first keeper of the Powder Magazine, built a house on Palace Street in the early 1700s. The house was later owned by William Dering, who was a painter and a dancing master. Neither Brush nor Dering belonged to the upper levels of society. Still, wealthy and well-known people came to Dering's classes. After all, the skill of dancing the minuet was very important to cultured British citizens when they attended social events and formal balls.[5]

By the middle of the seventeenth century, the Virginia colony had become a successful producer of tobacco. The gentry, or higher social classes, gained wealth and power.[6] They began to build elegant homes on plantations as well as in Williamsburg.

By about 1755, the Brush/Dering house belonged to Thomas Everard, a respected and wealthy citizen. He enlarged the house and added wood paneling and carvings to better reflect his position as a gentleman.[7] Today, visitors to the Thomas Everard House and other fine homes will see how the gentry lived.

## The George Wythe House

John Marshall (chief justice of the U.S. Supreme Court from 1801 to 1835) and Thomas Jefferson both studied law under

◄ George Wythe was a colonial lawyer and law professor. Visitors to Colonial Williamsburg can see his house where this reenactment of a woman using a spinning wheel is taking place.

George Wythe.[8] Wythe was a well-known lawyer and professor at the College of William and Mary. Today, people can visit Wythe's home, one of Williamsburg's grandest private residences.

During the Revolutionary War, General George Washington used the Wythe House as his headquarters. From there, Washington planned his attack on British forces at Yorktown (about twelve miles from Williamsburg).[9] After Washington's victory over British General Charles Cornwallis at the Battle of Yorktown, the British surrendered.

## The Governor's Palace

The Virginia colonists wanted their governor's home in Williamsburg to be the most elegant of all colonial mansions.[10] They started building it in 1706, but construction was delayed again and again to raise more money for the project.

In 1710, Alexander Spotswood became the governor of Virginia. He was eager to move into the mansion. In 1711, Governor Spotswood decorated the just-finished entry hall with an exhibit of fancy muskets. He not only pushed for the completion of his home-to-be, he insisted it be made more beautiful.[11]

About 1714, townspeople began calling the governor's home the "Palace."[12] The building lived up to its name. Years later, an admiring professor at the College of William and Mary described the house as "a magnificent Structure built at the publick Expense, finished and beautified with Gates, Fine Gardens, Offices, Walks, a fine Canal, Orchards. . . ."[13]

In 1716, Governor Spotswood moved into the home although it was not yet completed. The Governor's Palace was finished in 1722, and was home to many Virginia governors. Still, work went on.

Over the years, elegant gardens were planted. A new rear wing added a ballroom and supper room.[14] With its grand balls and fancy dinners, the Governor's Palace was the center of fashionable

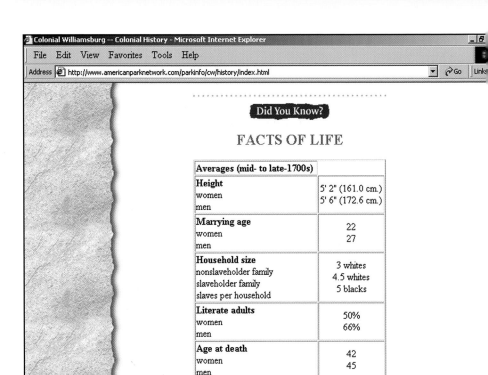

**Did You Know?**

## FACTS OF LIFE

| Averages (mid- to late-1700s) | |
|---|---|
| **Height**<br>women<br>men | 5' 2" (161.0 cm.)<br>5' 6" (172.6 cm.) |
| **Marrying age**<br>women<br>men | 22<br>27 |
| **Household size**<br>nonslaveholder family<br>slaveholder family<br>slaves per household | 3 whites<br>4.5 whites<br>5 blacks |
| **Literate adults**<br>women<br>men | 50%<br>66% |
| **Age at death**<br>women<br>men | 42<br>45 |

*This chart shows what the population was like in Colonial Williamsburg during the time of the American Revolution.*

society. Important representatives of other countries and American Indian tribes called on the governor there.[15]

The last British governor to live in the Governor's Palace was John Murray, Earl of Dunmore. After the uproar over the gunpowder theft from the Powder Magazine, Dunmore ordered marines to the Governor's Palace to protect him. He soon fled, leaving the Governor's Palace to the angry colonists.

## ▶ The Colonists and the Governor's Palace

The colonists pulled Spotswood's muskets from the walls of the Governor's Palace entry hall and put them to use in battle. They auctioned off Dunmore's private belongings, including furniture and African-American slaves. After the colonies declared their independence from Great Britain, Patrick Henry and Thomas Jefferson lived in the Governor's Palace.[16] While Jefferson was there, he drew a floor plan of the Governor's Palace and its gardens.[17]

During the Battle of Yorktown, the Governor's Palace was used as a hospital for American soldiers. That December, a fire destroyed the building. The government sold off the bricks and the remaining buildings.

Nearly 150 years later, archaeologists working for Colonial Williamsburg began uncovering the remains of the Governor's Palace. Based on all the information they could get, skilled workers rebuilt the Governor's Palace and replaced its furnishings. They used information from the archeologists, colonial records, Jefferson's drawings, and an engraving discovered in an English library.[18]

## ▶ Behind the Fine Homes

Not everybody got to enjoy the grand lifestyle on Palace Street or anywhere else in Williamsburg. Most Virginians lived in simpler houses or cabins. They worked at their crafts or trades with the help of family members, hired workers, or perhaps an indentured worker or African-American slave.

Many Europeans signed an agreement to work for someone else for a certain amount of time (usually five to twelve years) in return for passage on a ship to the New World. Called indentured servants, they did not have the right to quit their jobs, but they could eventually work off their time and be free.

The practice of slavery became a big commercial business after the New World was discovered. Then, large numbers of workers were needed for huge plantations. Almost all slaves in the American colonies were of African descent.

Some indentured servants and many African-American slaves made possible the comfortable lifestyles of wealthier families. On Palace Street and in other parts of Williamsburg, these workers lived behind the fine homes where they were employed. Homes

▲ *This painting shows what it may have been like when the first African slaves arrived in Jamestown. Many slaves lived in the Williamsburg colony as well.*

showing how and where these people lived are there today. Visitors can learn more about slavery from actors playing the roles of individuals who once lived in Williamsburg.

In 1775, more than half of the Williamsburg residents were African Americans.[19] Most of these African Americans were slaves. Williamsburg also had a small free African-American population. Actors also play those roles and answer questions about the lives of free African-American Virginians.[20]

# The Bell Rang Out for Freedom

**When** the Governor's Palace was finished in 1722, it soon became the center of social and political life for Virginia gentry. Over the next sixty years, though, attention shifted to another political center—the Capitol building.

As years went by, many Virginia colonists began to think of themselves as Virginians, rather than as British citizens. In the 1700s, some began thinking of themselves as Americans. At the Capitol, Virginians helped start the process that turned thirteen separate British colonies into one country.

## The Capitol Building

In 1701, Virginia colonists started building a Capitol at one end of Duke of Gloucester Street. Lawmakers moved into the Capitol in 1704, although it was not quite finished. Years later, the building was destroyed by fire and replaced by a different design. Many colonial records still existed that showed what the first building had looked like. Due to these records, the building that visitors see today looks like the original Capitol building.[1]

The Capitol has two wings, both of which are rounded on the front.

*Virginia's lawmakers began using the Capitol building in 1704. The building even held public hangings. The current building is the third building that has been put at that site.*

The General Assembly—the part of Virginia's government made up of colonists—met in the Capitol. The building also held offices, committee rooms, and the courtroom.

While the General Court met in the Capitol every April and October, the Court of Oyer and Terminer heard criminal cases there in June and December. ("Oyer and Terminer" means "to hear and to end.")[2] Punishments could be severe for convicted criminals. Burglars, pirates, horse thieves, forgers, and arsonists were often given the death penalty—usually by public hanging.[3] In 1779, during the Revolutionary War, the Virginia General Assembly limited the death sentence to a smaller range of offenses.[4]

## ▶ The Public Gaol

Just north of the Capitol, the Public Gaol (pronounced jail) held the accused until his or her trial. Sometimes the Public Gaol also held debtors, runaway slaves, and the mentally ill. During the Revolutionary War, captured British soldiers, loyalists, and accused traitors, spies, or deserters from the Continental Army were all kept in the Public Gaol.[5]

The prisoners were sometimes shackled—cuffed and chained by their ankles and/or wrists—in their cells. Today, the Public Gaol is open to visitors, who can see the cells and try on shackles.[6]

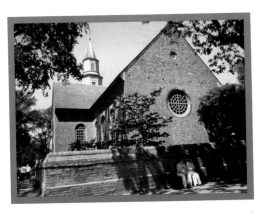

◁ The area that became the town of Williamsburg was once a plantation with a large church, called the Bruton Parish Church. The town was built around the church, which still holds religious services.

## Bruton Parish Church

Before the town of Williamsburg was renamed, there was a church at Middle Plantation. It was called Bruton Parish Church, named for a city in England. The town of Williamsburg grew around the community church and outgrew it by the early 1700s. The townspeople built a larger church, which has been in use since 1715.[7]

About 1755, Gaolkeeper Peter Pelham was hired to play the church's new English organ.[8] He would bring a prisoner from the Public Gaol to pump the air that flowed through the organ pipes.[9] In 1761, a merchant presented the church with a bell that is still in use. The townspeople added a new bell tower and a steeple. They often rang the church bell to alert citizens to important events.

Bruton Parish Church is on Duke of Gloucester Street at the corner of Palace Street. It is owned by and still holds services for an Episcopal congregation.

## The House of Burgesses

The Virginia colony was run by the governor and a two-part General Assembly. The General Assembly was made up of the Council and the House of Burgesses. Being a member of either

*Thomas Jefferson was the first secretary of state of the United States, as well as the third president. Jefferson was a Virginian who had served in the colony's House of Burgesses.*

part of the General Assembly was considered an honor.[10] Patrick Henry, George Washington, Thomas Jefferson, and other important Virginia leaders were members of the House of Burgesses in the years that led up to the American Revolution.

The Council was made up of colonists appointed by the British king. They generally supported the governor's decisions. Members of the House of Burgesses were elected by property-owning male colonists.[11] Burgesses often had their own ideas about how the colony should operate. They felt that, as British citizens, they had the right to make their own laws and set their own taxes.

## ▶ Governors and Burgesses Disagree

Members of the Virginia House of Burgesses were enraged by the Stamp Act, which Great Britain passed in 1765. This act said that colonists had to buy official stamps for all commercial and legal papers. Stamps had to be put on licenses, newspapers, pamphlets, almanacs, playing cards, dice, and liquor licenses.[12] Patrick Henry and other burgesses made angry speeches against the Stamp Act.

In response, Virginia Governor Francis Fauquier announced that the House of Burgesses was dissolved—that the members were out of a job. The burgesses obediently disbanded. Soon afterward, when Governor Fauquier held a birthday celebration for the British king, hardly anyone attended the party.[13] When Great Britain repealed the Stamp Act in 1776, the Bruton Parish Church bell rang to announce that victory.[14]

Other governors also dissolved the House of Burgesses over political disputes. Each time, this put an end to meetings in the Capitol. It was also supposed to put an end to discussions. However, the burgesses often simply refused to give up. Instead, they moved to a nearby tavern and continued their business.[15]

In December 1773, New England merchants were furious over new taxes on tea. In Massachusetts, merchants held a protest called the Boston Tea Party. They dressed like American Indians and dumped British tea into Boston Harbor. In early 1774, the British closed Boston Harbor as punishment for the deed.

The Virginia burgesses objected to the closing of Boston Harbor. They expressed their support for the Bostonians. This irritated Governor Dunmore, who dissolved the House of Burgesses in response.[16]

## The Raleigh Tavern

When the House of Burgesses was dissolved, most of its members went on with their work at the Raleigh Tavern.[17] First opened around 1717, the Raleigh Tavern is on Duke of Gloucester Street, near the Capitol. Virginia lawmakers met there so often that the tavern was sometimes called "the second capitol of the colony."[18]

The Raleigh Tavern was also a place to go for fine dinners, grand balls, exhibits, lectures, auctions, and various meetings. At the Raleigh Tavern today, actors play the roles of colonists.[19]

Located on Duke of Gloucester Street, the Raleigh Tavern became a meeting place for Virginia's lawmakers. When the building was reconstructed in 1926 it was Colonial Williamsburg's first building that tourists could visit.

Hungry visitors can buy cookies, cakes, and bread in the Raleigh Tavern Bake Shop.[20]

## The Burgesses Vote and the Bells Ring

In 1774, the Virginia House of Burgesses called a meeting at the Capitol to decide how to protest other British policies. This time, they voted to send delegates to a meeting called the Continental Congress, which was in Philadelphia. That was the first big step toward getting the colonies together.

In May 1776, the Bruton Parish Church bell rang as a daring resolution was announced. The resolution, passed by the House of Burgesses, called on the Continental Congress to declare independence from Great Britain.[21] In July, the Continental Congress did exactly that.

Virginian Thomas Jefferson wrote the Declaration of Independence. Jefferson and six other members of the Virginia House of Burgesses signed the document. George Washington did not sign it—but only because he was already busy leading the Continental Army. General Washington was preparing the Continental Army to fight the British for American independence.

Colonial Life
Continues

**From** 1699 to 1780, Williamsburg was the capital of Virginia. During the Revolutionary War, the Virginia capital was moved to Richmond, which was considered a safer location.[1] Richmond was also more centrally located since the Virginia population had grown and spread westward.

▲ This map shows the layout and major buildings in Colonial Williamsburg. Each larger building in this image represents a major tourist stop.

Even when it was no longer the state capital, Williamsburg was still a county seat (location of county government and courts). Students still came to the College of William and Mary to continue their education. Nearby farmers still brought their produce to the town market.

Williamsburg, though, was no longer the center of Virginia's social, cultural, and political life. It became a much quieter town. Some of the original buildings were destroyed. Others were added to and remodeled according to changing styles. Over the following century and a half, Williamsburg got a bit run-down.

## Rebirth of Colonial Life

Amazingly, the historic area of the town today looks very much like it did when it was the capital. All the buildings are colonial in style. Those open to the public are furnished with antiques or carefully made reproductions. Gardens like those of the eighteenth century are open to those who want to stroll through. Colonial-style taverns and restaurants still serve snacks and elegant meals. If visitors want, they can exchange modern money for "colonial money," and spend it in colonial-style shops for items like those sold there in days gone by.[2]

Historical interpreters in colonial dress go about life as people did in colonial days. They will talk to guests about what life was like back then. Costumed guides greet the visitors that come to Williamsburg every year. Being in Williamsburg is like taking a trip back in time.

## The Rector and the Philanthropist

In 1926, the rector of Bruton Parish Church was aware of Williamsburg's place in American history. Reverend W.A.R. Goodwin saw the town as a window to the past. However he knew that some of Williamsburg's windows would have to be restored for anyone to look through them.[3]

▲ *This painting called "Battle of Williamsburg" depicts that Civil War battle from 1862. Many of the original buildings in Williamsburg were destroyed by fire during that battle.*

Only a few Williamsburg buildings had been saved from destruction or change. In 1888, citizens had formed the Association for the Preservation of Virginia Antiquities (APVA) to buy and take care of the Powder Magazine.[4] Early in the twentieth century, Goodwin restored the inside of Bruton Parish Church to its eighteenth-century appearance.[5] However, many other buildings had disappeared or been changed beyond recognition.

In 1926, Goodwin talked with wealthy businessman and philanthropist John D. Rockefeller, Jr. Rockefeller agreed to support the project financially on the condition that it included the whole town.[6]

Rockefeller's project became the first major attempt to bring back an entire colonial town.[7] He did not only want to restore buildings. Rockefeller wanted to re-create the spirit of the town—to show life as it had been lived long ago.

## How Do You Put a Whole Town Back Together?

Rockefeller put a team of researchers, scientists, and workmen on the job. Maps, deeds, drawings, old photographs, and written accounts provided descriptions of some buildings. The most important discovery was an eighteenth-century copperplate found at the Bodleian Library at Oxford University in England. A copperplate is a polished sheet of copper with a drawing etched into its surface. Copperplates were used for printing the images engraved on them.

Architectural drawings of some of Williamsburg's most important buildings had been etched on the copperplate. The Bodleian Plate was used to reconstruct those buildings.[8]

Archeologists also went to work, digging in the Williamsburg ruins. They found the foundations of buildings like the Governor's Palace. From the foundations, they could tell where walls, steps, and doorways had been. The archeologists also turned up pieces of brick, stone, and tile that had been used in the original buildings. They found metal locks, keys, and hardware that had been on shutters and doors.[9]

Skilled designers, craftspeople, and workers put all these clues together and rebuilt an entire colonial town. Today, as the guidebook says, Williamsburg is the "world's oldest and largest living history museum."[10]

## The Colonial Williamsburg Foundation

From 1926 until his death in 1960 John D. Rockefeller, Jr., paid for the preservation of more than eighty buildings. He financed the reconstruction of many more. He also built accommodations for

(Courtesy of United Press International)

*John D. Rockefeller, Jr., was the only son of industrialist John D. Rockefeller. Rockefeller, Jr., financed the reconstruction of over eighty buildings in Colonial Williamsburg.*

visitors to the town. Rockefeller set up a foundation to carry on the job after his death.

The Colonial Williamsburg Foundation is a private, not-for-profit educational institution. The foundation continues to preserve and interpret the Williamsburg Historic Area, operate facilities for visitors, and sell accurate reproductions of colonial items. The foundation also supports history education in Williamsburg and in the public school system.[11]

In addition to the Williamsburg Historic Area, the Colonial Williamsburg Foundation operates several important museums.

## The Public Hospital and DeWitt Wallace Decorative Arts Museum

The Public Hospital is two blocks from Duke of Gloucester Street, on Francis Street. The hospital was built in 1773 for the care and treatment of the mentally ill. The building was badly damaged by fire in 1885, and was later rebuilt by the Colonial Williamsburg Foundation. Today, visitors can see how patients once lived and how they were treated according to medical practices and theories of the time.[12]

By going through the lower level of the Public Hospital, one can enter the DeWitt Wallace Decorative Arts Museum. The museum displays a wide range of British and American decorative arts, including furniture, metalwork, fabrics, costumes, and paintings. Special events include music and craft programs.[13] These collections and re-creations of events from earlier times help bring the history of Williamsburg to life.

## The Abby Aldrich Rockefeller Folk Art Museum

In 1939, Abby Aldrich Rockefeller, wife of John D. Rockefeller, Jr., gave her collection of American folk art to Colonial Williamsburg. Folk art is creative work done by everyday people, rather than by professional artists. Since then, the collection has grown through gifts and purchases. The exhibits include paintings, needlework, furniture, boxes, model ships, weather vanes, toys, shop signs, and decoys that date from the eighteenth century to the present.[14] The annual Christmas exhibition features popular toys, dollhouses, and a tree with handmade ornaments.[15]

## Carter's Grove

Six miles from the Williamsburg Historic Area is a restored plantation with a mansion house, agricultural areas, an orchard, slave quarters, and an archeological museum. Carter's Grove was the eighteenth-century estate of a wealthy Virginia family. Today, it

A tourist guide in a period costume educates visitors in Colonial Williamsburg. The town and townspeople make visitors feel as if they have actually gone back to colonial times.

provides a glimpse into plantation life. Archeologists also have uncovered evidence from those who lived on this land before Carter's Grove was built. Those items are on display in the archeological museum.[16]

## Why Travel Back in Time?

Colonial Williamsburg provides many opportunities for recreation. In the summers and on special weekends, young people can learn colonial dances, participate in games, and help with activities such as gardening.[17] Boys and girls also can rent and wear eighteenth-century costumes.[18] Williamsburg, though, is more than things to see and games to play.

Williamsburg is a living example of American life before the creation of the United States. It is where some colonial leaders first thought about—and spoke out about—breaking away from Great Britain and starting a new country. It will also always be known as the place where some ideals of the new nation were first put into words and action.

**archaeologists**—Scientists who study the remains of older cultures, such as buildings, graves, and tools, to learn about the people of that time.

**bayonet**—A blade, usually made of steel, attached to the end of a rifle for hand-to-hand combat.

**cask**—A barrel-shaped container used for holding liquid, usually wine.

**foundry**—An establishment where metals are shaped.

**indentured servant**—A person who works for another for a specific amount of time in return for payment of travel and basic living expenses.

**loyalist**—In Colonial times, a person who remained loyal to the British government and the king of England.

**militia**—A group of local volunteer citizens organized for military service that is not the official army of the land.

**milliner**—A person who designs, makes, trims, or sells women's hats.

**minuet**—Slow, flowing dance in three-quarter time in which dancers do a lot of forward balancing, bowing, and toe pointing.

**musket**—A gun with a long barrel that is fired from the shoulder. Muskets are loaded from the front, called the muzzle. Muskets were used between the sixteenth and eighteenth centuries, before rifles were invented.

**philanthropist**—A person who contributes to the welfare of others without an obligation.

**pillory**—Wooden device with holes in which a person's head and hands were locked; used to publicly punish an offender.

**rector**—A clergyman or clergywoman responsible for an entire parish.

**steeple**—Church tower.

**whipping post**—Post to which offenders are tied so that they can be whipped in punishment.

## Chapter 1. The Sword Is Drawn!

1. The Colonial Williamsburg Foundation, "Magazine," *See the Places: Historic Sites & Buildings,* © 2003, <http://www.history.org/Almanack/places/hb/hbmag.cfm> (November 4, 2003).

2. Ibid.

3. Ibid.

4. Ibid.

5. Naval Documents of the American Revolution (NDAR), vol. 1, *"Purdie's Virginia Gazette,* Friday, April 21, 1775," *Primary Documents Relating to the Seizure of Powder at Williamsburg, VA, April 21, 1775,* n.d., <http://www.revwar75.com/battles/primarydocs/williamsburg.htm> (November 4, 2003).

6. Ibid.

7. APN Media, LLC, "Colonial Williamsburg History: Colonial History," *American Park Network,* © 2001, <http://www.americanparknetwork.com/parkinfo/cw/history/> (November 4, 2003).

8. The Colonial Williamsburg Foundation, "Magazine," *See the Places: Historic Sites & Buildings,* © 2003, <http://www.history.org/Almanack/places/hb/hbmag.cfm> (November 4, 2003).

9. Ibid.

10. Ibid.

11. Michael Olmert, *Official Guide to Colonial Williamsburg* (Williamsburg, Va.: The Colonial Williamsburg Foundation, 1998), pp. 27, 30.

12. Ibid., p. 41.

13. Ibid., p. 37.

14. Ibid., p. 39.

15. Alice Morse Earle, *Curious Punishments of Bygone Days* (New York: Macmillan, 1896), p. 18.

16. Olmert, p. 40.

17. Ibid., p. 27.

18. Ibid., pp. 37–38.

## Chapter 2. Everyday Life on the Great Street

1. Michael Olmert, *Official Guide to Colonial Williamsburg* (Williamsburg, Va.: The Colonial Williamsburg Foundation, 1998), p. 81.

2. APN Media, LLC, "Colonial Williamsburg History: Colonial History," *American Park Network,* © 2001, <http://www.americanparknetwork.com/parkinfo/cw/history/> (November 4, 2003).

3. Ibid.

4. The Colonial Williamsburg Foundation, "Duke of Gloucester Street," *See the Places: Historic Sites & Buildings,* © 2003, <http://www.history.org/Almanack/places/hb/hbduke.cfm> (November 4, 2003).

5. Olmert, p. 64.

6. The Colonial Williamsburg Foundation, "Duke of Gloucester Street."

7. Ibid.

8. A. Lawrence Kocher and Howard Dearstyne, *Colonial Williamsburg: Its Buildings and Gardens* (Williamsburg: Colonial Williamsburg, Inc., 1949), p. 87.

9. The Colonial Williamsburg Foundation, "Wren Building," *See the Places: Historic Sites & Buildings,* © 2003, <http://www.history.org/Almanack/places/hb/hbwren.cfm> (November 4, 2003).

10. Olmert, pp. 99–100.

11. The Colonial Williamsburg Foundation, "Wren Building."

12. Olmert, p. 100.

13. Kocher and Dearstyne, pp. 8–9.

14. The Colonial Williamsburg Foundation, "Wren Building."

## Chapter 3. British Nobility and Virginia Gentry

1. APN Media, LLC, "Colonial Williamsburg History: Colonial History," *American Park Network,* © 2001, <http://www.americanparknetwork.com/parkinfo/cw/history/> (November 4, 2003).

2. Ibid.

3. The Colonial Williamsburg Foundation, "Palace Green," *See the Places: Historic Sites & Buildings,* © 2003, <http://www.history.org/Almanack/places/hb/hbpalgr.cfm> (November 5, 2003).

4. A. Lawrence Kocher and Howard Dearstyne, *Colonial Williamsburg: Its Buildings and Gardens* (Williamsburg: Colonial Williamsburg, Inc., 1949), p. 9.

5. Michael Olmert, *Official Guide to Colonial Williamsburg* (Williamsburg, Va.: The Colonial Williamsburg Foundation, 1998), p. 74.

6. APN Media, LLC, "Colonial Williamsburg History: Colonial History."

7. Olmert, p. 75.

8. Ibid., p. 79.

9. Ibid., p. 78.

10. Kocher and Dearstyne, pp. 50–53.

11. Olmert, p. 82.

12. The Colonial Williamsburg Foundation, "Governor's Palace," *See the Places: Historic Sites & Buildings,* © 2003, <http://www.history.org/Almanack/places/hb/hbpal.cfm> (November 4, 2003).

13. Ibid.

14. Olmert, p. 84.

15. The Colonial Williamsburg Foundation, "Governor's Palace."

16. Ibid.

17. Ibid.

18. Ibid.

19. Olmert, p. 125.

20. Ibid.

## Chapter 4. The Bell Rang Out for Freedom

1. Michael Olmert, *Official Guide to Colonial Williamsburg* (Williamsburg, Va.: The Colonial Williamsburg Foundation, 1998), p. 63.

2. Ibid.

3. Ibid.

4. Thomas Jefferson, *Autobiography: Writings,* Merrill D. Peterson, ed. (New York: Library Classics of the United States, 1984), p. 39.

5. Olmert. p. 67.

6. Ibid., p. 32.

7. Ibid., p. 94.

8. Ibid., p. 68.

9. The Colonial Williamsburg Foundation, "Bruton Parish Church," *See the Places: Historic Sites & Buildings,* © 2003, <http://www.history.org/Almanack/places/hb/hbbruch.cfm> (November 4, 2003).

10. APN Media, LLC, "Colonial Williamsburg History: Colonial History," *American Park Network,* © 2001, <http://www.americanparknetwork.com/parkinfo/cw/history/> (November 4, 2003).

11. Olmert, p. 61.

12. Richard Hofstadter, William Miller, and Daniel Aaron, *The United States: The History of a Republic* (Englewood Cliffs, N.J.: Prentice-Hall, 1957), p. 92.

13. The Colonial Williamsburg Foundation, "Governor's Palace," *See the Places: Historic Sites & Buildings,* © 2003, <http://www.history.org/Almanack/places/hb/hbpal.cfm> (November 4, 2003).

14. A. Lawrence Kocher and Howard Dearstyne, *Colonial Williamsburg: Its Buildings and Gardens* (Williamsburg: Colonial Williamsburg, Inc., 1949), p. vi.

15. The Colonial Williamsburg Foundation, "Raleigh Tavern," *See the Places: Historic Sites & Buildings,* © 2003, <http://www.history.org/Almanack/places/hb/hbral.cfm> (November 4, 2003).

16. APN Media, LLC, "Colonial Williamsburg History: Colonial History."

17. The Colonial Williamsburg Foundation, "Raleigh Tavern."

18. Kocher and Dearstyne, p. 65.

19. Olmert, p. 28.

20. Ibid., p. 155.

21. Kocher and Dearstyne, p. vi.

## Chapter 5. Colonial Life Continues

1. Michael Olmert, *Official Guide to Colonial Williamsburg* (Williamsburg, Va.: The Colonial Williamsburg Foundation, 1998), p. 21.

2. Ibid., p. 12.

3. Ibid., p. 22.

4. The Colonial Williamsburg Foundation, "Magazine," *See the Places: Historic Sites & Buildings,* © 2003, <http://www.history.org/Almanack/places/hb/hbmag.cfm> (November 4, 2003).

5. Olmert, p. 94.

6. Ibid., p. 22.

7. A. Lawrence Kocher and Howard Dearstyne, *Colonial Williamsburg: Its Buildings and Gardens* (Williamsburg: Colonial Williamsburg, Inc., 1949), p. 43.

8. Olmert, p. 23.

9. Ibid.

10. Ibid.

11. The Colonial Williamsburg Foundation, "The History of Colonial Williamsburg," © 2003, <http://www.history.org/Foundation/cwhistory.cfm> (November 5, 2003).

12. Olmert, pp. 133–134.

13. Ibid., pp. 135–136.

14. Ibid., pp. 138–139.

15. The Colonial Williamsburg Foundation, "The Abby Aldrich Rockefeller Folk Art Museum," *Colonial Williamsburg Museums,* © 2002,<http://www.georgetown.u47.k12.me.us/history/museums/abby_art.cfm> (November 4, 2003).

16. Olmert, pp. 140–146.

17. Ibid., p. 32.

18. Ibid.

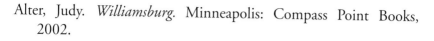
Alter, Judy. *Williamsburg.* Minneapolis: Compass Point Books, 2002.

Day, Nancy. *Your Travel Guide to Colonial America.* Minneapolis: Runestone Press, 2001.

DeCapua, Sarah E. *The Virginia Colony.* Chanhassen, Minn.: Child's World, 2003.

Green, Carl R. *The Revolutionary War.* Berkeley Heights, N.J.: MyReportLinks.com Books, 2002.

Kalman, Bobbie, and John Crossingham. *Colonial Home.* New York: Crabtree Publishing, 2001.

Kukla, Amy, and Jon. *Patrick Henry: Voice of the Revolution.* New York: PowerKids Press Books, 2002.

McCarthy, Pat. *The Thirteen Colonies From Founding to Revolution.* Berkeley Heights, N.J.: Enslow Publishers, Inc., 2004.

O'Connell, Kimberly A. *Virginia.* Berkeley Heights, N.J.: MyReportLinks.com Books, 2003.

Samuel, Charlie. *Government and Politics in Colonial America.* New York: PowerKids Press, 2003.

Schomp, Virginia. *The Revolutionary War.* New York: Benchmark Books, 2003.

Stefoff, Rebecca. *Colonial Life.* New York: Benchmark Books, 2003.

Steins, Richard. *Colonial America.* Austin, Tex.: Raintree Steck-Vaughn, 2000.

Walker, Niki. *Colonial Women.* New York: Crabtree Publishers, 2003.